Henry & James Go Fishing

ISBN: 978-1-969463-30-3

To my sons, who are the inspiration for these characters.

John, your resilience, thirst for knowledge, curiosity, and incredible stories make you a true gift.

James and David, your unconditional love, support, and patience with your brother have shaped the men you have become: patient with yourselves and others, as well as accepting of everyone, especially those who are different in their own unique ways.

To every mother, father, family member, and friend of someone on the Autism Spectrum, you are brave, caring, supported, seen, and heard, and so are your loved ones.

"Wake up, wake up! What a lovely day!"
Came Mama's voice from far away.
He tosses and turns, warm in his bed.
She cannot rouse her sleepyhead.

Shutters swing open, the room's
bathed in light He peeks from his
covers, Mama's nowhere in sight!
He yawns and stretches, hearing
pots and pans drumming, Jumps
out of his bed to the sound of
Mom's humming.

"Good morning, Henry," Mom says cheerfully.
Young Henry smiles, raising James up to see.
"I almost forgot, good morning to James,"
She pats him lightly, playing young Henry's
game.

James, as you see, is Henry's best mate,
An elephant stuffed, and to Henry he's great!
His blue fluff all matted, his big ears like rings,
Eyes of blue gems and a smile made of string.

Henry sits at the table with James at his side, Awaiting their breakfast, watching Mama with pride. "It's a warm day, Mama, and I was just wishing. Could me and James, please, spend the day going fishing?"

Mama chuckles and smiles as she looks at the pool, "I guess that's okay, yeah, I think that sounds cool." Henry's grin grows wider as she sets down his eggs Excitedly naming the fish he will bag.

As Henry finishes breakfast,
big brother comes in. "Morning,
William," he says, "did you sleep
in?" William ruffles his hair and
pats his brother, "Yes, but
something smells great.
Where's breakfast, Mother?"

A plate of his favorite—eggs, bacon, and toast, He thanks Mama sweetly, stating he loves her most. This got Henry thinking how to make Mama proud: Catch a whole bunch of fish, perhaps a whole crowd!

"I'm going to get ready," he yells from the door.
"Don't forget James and sunscreen," came Mama's roar.
"Oh yeah, I remember," Henry replies.
"It's cold," he giggles as the sunscreen's applied.

Finally free to head out and gather his gear,
With James, hat and pole, and a towel dragging rear.
"Where is he off to?" William asks, looking leery.
"He's going fishing," Mama sighs, sounding weary.

"Please keep an eye on him, for his own good,"
Mama smiles at William gently, lifting the mood.
"I'll make sure there's fresh water and the pool is all
clean." He says as he kisses her, feeling wiser and keen.

See, Henry is different, even though he's now seven, He's got special quirks, Mama's sweetheart from Heaven, He has good days and bad; he'll get better with time. Autism, it's called; and it's all God's design.

For now, he's surrounded in his family's embrace, No special treatment, growing up is no race! He's a little bit slower, but his humor is sharp, His brain like a sponge; he is clever and smart.

Henry needs extra watching; he's forgetful at times, But his family accepts him without any whines. So William, now 12, sets out to the yard. A warm summer day, watching Henry's not hard.

William brings the hose over; the pool needs refilling. He smiles when he glimpses Henry, James, and gear milling. "Hey, kiddo," he calls, "blow your boat up with air." "See how fast you can do it," he laughs, "if you dare."

Henry puckers his lips, his cheeks and eyes bulging, Determined to do it, he needs no cajoling. His face turns bright red as the air whooshes out. William grabs his sides laughing while young Henry pouts.

"It's okay, little brother, you gave a good try." Henry's lower lip quivers—he looks ready to cry. William kneels down beside him, his arms open wide, He tucks Henry in for a hug filled with pride

"Go on— Grab the tire pump," William directs. Off Henry goes to the shed to collect. Back in a flash, all excited and flushed. "Hurry up now, William," Henry whoops, sounding rushed.

"All ready to go," William says with a smile.
"Be careful, little bro, watch out for crocodiles."
Henry just shakes his head as he gathers his tackle,
"You've got a lot to learn, brother," Henry chortles
and cackles.

The boat's in the pool with James, towel, and gear.
Henry clambers onboard and sits in the rear.
"Now, don't go too far. I'll be watching from shore."
William warns his brother as he hands him the oars.

Their big swimming pool is the perfect spot
To relax and have fun when the sun is so hot!
To Henry, of course, it's THE only place for all his
adventures through time and through space.

Today, as he rows to the big pool's center
He imagines the pond and the world he will enter.
The surrounding patio becomes lush and green—
A beautiful landscape that's truly serene.

The crickets are chirping, and the nearby frogs croak,
Water bugs gracefully dance a backstroke.
A warm summer breeze rustles the trees
And birds softly sing 'bout the buzzing of bees.

"This looks to be it," young Henry proclaims
As he sets down the oars and gets ready to aim.
He takes up his pole and casts out his line
With James by his side, now he waits for a sign.

"The fish will start biting," he states, full of hope
As he and James wait for the tug of the rope.
"I'll bet you there's salmon, that's always Mom's
favorite. Or big rainbow trout or even some halibut."

Henry and James continue to wait,
Searching the tackle for just the right bait.
He hoists out the line to get a good look,
Then places a worm on the end of the hook.

Re-casting the hook with the fat juicy worm,
Henry sees James enthusiastically squirm.
"It won't be long now, we'll catch something
soon." As the weather starts changing, "Oh no,
a monsoon!"

The wind starts to blow, howling with rage,
Their boat gets tossed as the waves rampage.
"James! Hold on!" Henry cries o'er the storm
As the rain falls in sheets, their nice day transforms.

"Quick, grab the pole, don't let it get lost!"
They dive for the line as the boat gets storm-tossed.
Planting his feet against the side of the boat,
Henry steadies the rocking so they'll stay afloat.

"Fasten your life vest, make sure it is snug!"
He reminds his mate James as he gives it a tug.
The waves grow higher as they rock to and fro,
They pitch and they sway like a giant yo-yo.

They hold on tight to each other in terror.
"I will not be a bad news bearer!"
"Mama will get her fish," young Henry shouts.
"The storm will soon pass, it will soon peter out!"

Henry is right as the waves start to calm.
He lets go of James to wipe sweaty palms.
The clouds soon disperse, and out pops the sun, "Let's
get back to fishing and catch a whole ton!"

With a laugh and a giggle to steady the nerves,
The two young fishermen sit down to observe.
Watching the line as it bobs up and down,
Henry looks over to see his friend frown.

"What's wrong, James?' Henry asks with concern. "Did I
miss something? Would you like a turn?" James starts to
smile as Henry changes position, Helping James cast his
line with ambition.

The two of them sigh, but pay close attention.
Checking their line for the slightest of tension.
They hear a 'kerplop' and see water splashing,
And notice how shiny the silver is flashing.

"Looky there, James, a fish off the prow.
It looks gigantic—we'll catch it somehow!
Let's just be patient and hope that it's hungry.
Our fat, juicy worm is the perfect bribery.
It can't resist a sweet, tasty snack,
And so it will bite—its big lips will smack.
As soon as its jaw is secure on the hook,
We'll haul that fish in and get ready to cook!"

The fish makes a turn and swims under the boat,
While Henry and James excitedly gloat.
Swiftly it swims and its jaws open wide—
Nabbing the bait—it jerks with fierce pride.

The two young fishermen are caught off guard.
The line goes taut, tossing James aside, hard.
"Hold on, James, don't let go of the pole!"
Henry yells to his friend as he grabs for control.

Straining and stretching, Henry sets to the chore,
As a battle ensues, they play tug-of-war.
Henry is reeling with all of his might,
While James gets the net to help end the fight.

With a huff and a puff and one final hard pull,
The fish soon emerges—big and beautiful.
"Wow! This one's huge!" young Henry yelps.
"Hold the net steady, James, please help!"

The two friends manage with one final tug,
Ensnaring the fish in the net—nice and snug.
"Quick, grab the bucket. Let's put him in."
They happily whoop and excitedly grin.

Time to pack up and head back to shore.
They set to the task and each grab an oar.
It's late afternoon as the shore comes in sight.
"Let's get our fish home," Henry says with delight.

Tired and hungry, they gather their gear.
Departing the boat, "Hey, kiddo!" they hear.
"You've been gone quite a while," William states as he sits.
"What have you got? Where are your fish?"

Henry giggles and smiles, "Is Mama inside?"
With a nod of his head, William watches with pride.
As young Henry struggles to carry the weight,
William lends him a hand, taking tackle and bait.

"Mama, I'm back!" Henry hollers with glee,
As he strides 'cross the yard with much jubilee.
"My goodness," says Mama, as she stands in the
door. "What have we here? Are the crew all
ashore?"

"I've brought supper home that me and James
caught." Mama grins, looking puzzled, and asks,
"What ya got?" "A fish! See, I told you. A big
Rainbow Trout.
I'll help Daddy clean it and throw the guts out."

Later that evening, as Dad barbecues,
William, Henry, and James play with Henry's toy
zoo. Mama looks thoughtful as she ponders the
pool… Fish live in rivers or lakes as a rule.

As they sit down to dinner to enjoy the grilled trout, Mama thanks young Henry, but sees a small pout. "It's delicious fish, Henry, thank you, but you seem a bit sad." "You're right, Mama, it's great! But, let me just add..."

Henry gets quiet as Mama leans in. "I'm just planning tomorrow," he says with a grin. From under the table, he pulls a toy lion. "Great day for safari," he smiles as he hears Mama sighing.

Francine Hatley

About the Author

Francine Hatley was born in Seattle, WA. When she was 5 years old her family settled in Richland, WA. After graduating high school, she went on to attend Seattle University earning a degree in English Literature with an emphasis on British Romanticism and Creative Writing. Francine married her high school sweetheart. They have 3 sons and one daughter-in-law, and currently reside in Arlington WA along with their 2 dogs, 2 cats and several chickens.

Dan & Nancy Schier

About the Illustrators

Daniel and Nancy Schier first met in 1999 while creating movies at Disney Feature Animation. Today, they love combining their talents—Daniel brings the characters into focus, and Nancy brings them to life with color and magic. It's hard to summarize their vast artistic interests and professional experiences, but suffice it to say, when they work together, they're quite the powerhouse! Of all their wide artistic adventures, their favorite projects are the stories they create together...
and their two wonderful children.